A LITTLE
TREASURY
OF GOLD

FOR YOU WITH LOVE

COMPILED BY
KAY ANNE CARSON

INSPIRATIONAL PRESS
NEW YORK

FOR MY ONE AND ONLY DAD
AND VERY FIRST VALENTINE,
ARTHUR J. ROCHE, WITH LOVE

Copyright © 1995 by Budget Book Service, Inc.

Published in 1995 by
INSPIRATIONAL PRESS
A division of Budget Book Service, Inc.
386 Park Avenue South
New York, NY 10016

Inspirational Press is a registered trademark
of Budget Book Service, Inc.

Library of Congress Catalog Card Number: 94-77198
ISBN: 0-88486-105-8

Designed by Cindy LaBreacht.
Printed in Hong Kong.

ACKNOWLEDGEMENTS

The compiler and publisher have made every effort to trace the ownership of all copyrighted poems. While expressing regret for any error unintentionally made, the publisher will be pleased to make the necessary correction in future editions of the book.

Sincere thanks are due the following publishers for cooperation in allowing the use of poems selected from their publications:

Doubleday & Company, Inc. for "I Am a Book I Neither Wrote Nor Read" from *Summer Knowledge* by Delmore Schwartz, copyright © 1959 by Delmore Schwartz. Reprinted by permission of the publisher.

Harper & Row Publishers, Inc. for "Love is not all: it is not meat nor drink" from *Collected Poems*, by Edna St. Vincent Millay, published by Harper & Row, copyright 1921, 1922, 1923, 1931, 1948, 1950, 1951, © 1958 by Edna St. Vincent Millay and Norma Millay Ellis. Reprinted by permission of the publisher.

Houghton Mifflin Company for "A Gift" from *The Complete Poetical Works of Amy Lowell*. Copyright © 1955 by Houghton Mifflin Company. Copyright © 1983 renewed by Houghton Mifflin Company, Brinton P. Roberts, Esquire and G. D'Andelot Belin, Esquire. Reprinted by permission of the publisher.

Little, Brown and Company Inc. for "No Time to Hate" reprinted by permission of the publishers, the Trustees of Amherst College and Little, Brown and Company Inc. from *The Complete Poems of Emily Dickinson*, ed. Thomas H. Johnson, Cambridge, Mass.: The Belknap Press of Harvard University Press, Copyright 1929 by Martha Dickinson Bianchi, copyright © renewed 1957 by Mary L. Hampson; Copyright © 1951, 1955, 1979, 1983 by the President and Fellows of Harvard College.

The Swallow Press, Inc., Chicago, for "And I Am Old to Know" from *Forever Young and Other Poems*, by Pauline Hanson. Reprinted by permission of the publisher.

CONTENTS

SONNET

My Love, I have no fear that thou shouldst die;
   Albeit I ask no fairer life than this,
Whose numbering-clock is still thy gentle kiss,
While Time and Peace with hands unlocked fly,–
   Yet care I not where in Eternity
We live and love, well knowing that there is
No backward step for those who feel the bliss
Of Faith as their most lofty yearnings high:
   Love hath so purified my being's core,
Meseems I scarcely should be startled, even,
To find, some morn, that thou hadst gone before;
Since, with thy love, this knowledge too was given,
Which each calm day doth strengthen more and more,
That they who love are but one step from Heaven.

JAMES RUSSELL LOWELL

I.

Love
hath
echoes
truer far

ECHOES

How sweet the answer Echo makes
To music at night
When, roused by lute or horn, she wakes,
And far away o'er lawns and lakes
Goes answering light!

Yet love hath echoes truer far
And far more sweet
Than e'er, beneath the moonlight's star,
Of horn or lute or soft guitar
The songs repeat.

'T is when the sigh—in youth sincere
And only then,
The sigh that's breathed for one to hear—
Is by that one, that only Dear
Breathed back again.

THOMAS MOORE

SHALL I COMPARE THEE TO A SUMMER'S DAY?

Shall I compare thee to a summer's day?
Thou art more lovely and more temperate:
Rough winds do shake the darling buds of May,
And summer's lease hath all too short a date;
Sometime too hot the eye of heaven shines,
And often is his gold complexion dimm'd;
And every fair from fair sometime declines,
By chance or nature's changing course untrimm'd:
But thy eternal summer shall not fade
Nor lose possession of that fair thou ow'st;
Nor shall Death brag thou wand'rest in his shade,
When in eternal lines to time thou grow'st;
So long as men can breathe or eyes can see,
So long lives this, and this gives life to thee.

WILLIAM SHAKESPEARE

MEETING

The gray sea, and the long black land;
And the yellow half-moon large and low;
And the startled little waves, that leap
In fiery ringlets from their sleep,
As I gain the cove with pushing prow,
And quench its speed in the slushy sand.

Then a mile of warm, sea-scented beach;
Three fields to cross, till a farm appears:
A tap at the pane, the quick sharp scratch
And blue spurt of a lighted match,
And a voice less loud, through its joy and fears,
Than the two hearts, beating each to each.

ROBERT BROWNING

WHY, LOVELY CHARMER!
FROM "THE HIVE"

Why, lovely charmer, tell me why,
So very kind, and yet so shy?
Why does that cold, forbidding air
Give damps of sorrow and despair?
Or why that smile my soul subdue,
And kindle up my flames anew?

In vain you strive with all your art,
By turns to fire and freeze my heart;
When I behold a face so fair,
So sweet a look, so soft an air,
My ravished soul is charmed all o'er,
I cannot love thee less or more.

AUTHOR UNKNOWN

THE SIESTA

Airs, that wander and murmur round,
Bearing delight where'er ye blow!
Make in the elms a lulling sound,
While my lady sleeps in the shade below.

Lighten and lengthen her noonday rest,
Till the heat of the noonday sun is o'er.
Sweet be her slumbers! though in my breast
The pain she has waked may slumber no more.
Breathing soft from the blue profound,
Bearing delight where'er ye blow,
Make in the elms a lulling sound,
While my lady sleeps in the shade below.

Airs! that over the bending boughs,
And under the shade of pendent leaves,
Murmur soft, like my timid vows
Or the secret sighs my bosom heaves,–
Gently sweeping the grassy ground,
Bearing delight where'er ye blow,
Make in the elms a lulling sound,
While my lady sleeps in the shade below.

WILLIAM CULLEN BRYANT

SHE IS NOT FAIR
TO OUTWARD VIEW

She is not fair to outward view,
As many maidens be;
Her loveliness I never knew
Until she smiled on me:
O, then I saw her eye was bright,–
A well of love, a spring of light.

But now her looks are coy and cold;
To mine they ne'er reply;
And yet I cease not to behold,
The love-light in her eye:
Her very frowns are better far
Than smiles of other maidens are!

HARTLEY COLERIDGE

AT THE CHURCH GATE

Although I enter not,
Yet round about the spot
Ofttimes I hover;
And near the sacred gate,
With longing eyes I wait,
Expectant of her.

The minster bell tolls out
Above the city's rout,
And noise and humming;
They've hushed the minster bell;
The organ 'gins to swell;
She's coming, coming!

My lady comes at last,
Timid and stepping fast,
And hastening hither,
With modest eyes downcast;
She comes,—she's here, she's past!
May Heaven go with her!

Kneel undisturbed, fair saint!
Pour out your praise or plaint
Meekly and duly;
I will not enter there,
To sully your pure prayer
With thoughts unruly.

But suffer me to pace
Round the forbidden place,
Lingering a minute,
Like outcast spirits, who wait,
And see, through heaven's gate,
Angels within it.

WILLIAM MAKEPEACE THACKERAY

LONGING

Come to me in my dreams, and then
By day I shall be well again!
For then the night will more than pay
The hopeless longing of the day.

Come, as thou cam'st a thousand times,
A messenger from radiant climes,
And smile on thy new world, and be
As kind to others as to me!

Or, as thou never cam'st in sooth,
Come now, and let me dream it truth;
And part my hair, and kiss my brow,
And say: *My love! why sufferest thou?*

Come to me in my dreams, and then
By day I shall be well again!
For then the night will more than pay
The hopeless longing of the day.

MATTHEW ARNOLD

I AM A BOOK I NEITHER WROTE NOR READ

I am a book I neither wrote nor read,
A comic, tragic play in which new masquerades
Astonishing as guns crackle like raids
Newly each time, whatever one is prepared
To come upon, suddenly dismayed and afraid,
As in the dreams which make the fear of sleep
The terror of love, the depth one cannot leap.

How the false truths of the years of youth have passed!
Have passed at full speed like trains which never stopped
There where I stood and waited, hardly aware,
How little I knew, or which of them was the one
To mount and ride to hope or where true hope arrives.

I no more wrote than read that book which is
The self I am, half-hidden as it is
From one and all who see within a kiss
The lounging formless blackness of an abyss.

How could I think the brief years were enough
To prove the reality of endless love?

DELMORE SCHWARTZ

THE LIGHT OF LOVE

Each shining light above us
Has its own peculiar grace;
But every light of heaven
Is in my darling's face.

For it is like the sunlight,
So strong and pure and warm,
That folds all good and happy things,
And guards from gloom and harm.

And it is like the moonlight,
So holy and so calm;
The rapt peace of a summer night,
When soft winds die in balm.

And it is like the starlight;
For, love her as I may,
She dwells still lofty and serene
In mystery far away.

JOHN HAY

A LOVE SONG

By the fierce flames of Love I'm in a sad taking,
I'm singed like a pig that is hung up for bacon,
My stomach is scorched like an over-done mutton-chop,
That for want of gravy wont afford a single drop.
Love, love, love is like a dizziness,
Wont let a poor man go about his business.

My great toes and little toes are burnt to a cinder,
As a hot burning-glass burns a dish-cloth to tinder,
As cheese by a hot salamander is roasted,
By beauty that's red-hot, like a cheese am I toasted.
Love, love, love is like a dizziness,
Wont let a-poor man go about his business.

Attend all young lovers, who after ladies dandle,
I'm singed like a duck's foot over a candle,
By this that and t'other, I'm treated uncivil,
Like a gizzard I'm peppered, and then made a devil.
Love, love, love is like a dizziness,
Wont let a poor man go about his business.

ROYALL TYLER

ECHO

I asked of Echo, t'other day
(Whose words are often few and funny),
What to a novice she could say
Of courtship, love, and matrimony.
Quoth Echo plainly,–"Matter-o'-money!"

Whom should I marry? Should it be
A dashing damsel, gay and pert,
A pattern of inconstancy;
Or selfish, mercenary flirt?
Quoth Echo, sharply,–"Nary flirt!"

What if, aweary of the strife
That long has lured the dear deceiver,
She promise to amend her life,
And sin no more; can I believe her?
Quoth Echo, very promptly,–"Leave her!"

But if some maiden with a heart
On me should venture to bestow it,
Pray, should I act the wiser part
To take the treasure or forego it?
Quoth Echo, with decision,–"Go it!"

But what if, seemingly afraid
To bind her fate in Hymen's fetter,
She vow she means to die a maid,
In answer to my loving letter?
Quoth Echo, rather coolly,–"Let her!"

What if, in spite of her disdain,
I find my heart intwined about
With Cupid's dear delicious chain
So closely that I can't get out?
Quoth Echo, laughingly,–"Get out!"

But if some maid with beauty blest,
As pure and fair as Heaven can make her,
Will share my labor and my rest
Till envious Death shall overtake her?
Quoth Echo (sotto voce),–"Take her!"

JOHN GODFREY SAXE

II.

Such
I believe
my love

IF IT BE TRUE THAT ANY BEAUTEOUS THING

If it be true that any beauteous thing
Raises the pure and just desire of man
From earth to God, the eternal fount of all,
Such I believe my love; for as in her
So fair, in whom I all besides forget,
I view the gentle work of her Creator,
I have no care for any other thing,
Whilst thus I love. Nor is it marvellous,
Since the effect is not of my own power,
If the soul doth, by nature tempted forth,
Enamored through the eyes,
Repose upon the eyes which it resembleth,
And through them riseth to the Primal Love,
As to its end, and honors in admiring;
For who adores the Maker needs must love his work.

MICHAELANGELO
TRANSLATION OF J. E. TAYLOR

IF THOU MUST LOVE ME

If thou must love me, let it be for naught
Except for love's sake only. Do not say
"I love her for her smile...her look...her way
Of speaking gently,—for a trick of thought
That falls in well with mine, and certes brought
A sense of pleasant ease on such a day."
For these things in themselves, beloved, may
Be changed, or change for thee,—and love so wrought,
May be unwrought so. Neither love me for
Thine own dear pity's wiping my cheeks dry,—
A creature might forget to weep, who bore
Thy comfort long, and lose thy love thereby.
But love me for love's sake, that evermore
Thou mayst love on, through love's eternity.

ELIZABETH BARRETT BROWNING

THE PASSIONATE SHEPHERD
TO HIS LOVE

Come live with me and my love,
And we will all the pleasures prove
That valleys, groves, hills, and fields,
Woods, or steepy mountain yields.

And we will sit upon the rocks,
Seeing the shepherds feed their flocks
By shallow rivers, to whose falls
Melodious birds sing madrigals.

And I will make thee beds of roses
And a thousand fragrant posies;
A cap of flowers and a kirtle
Embroidered all with leaves of myrtle;

A gown made of the finest wool
Which from our pretty lambs we pull;
Fair lined slippers for the cold,
With buckles of the purest gold;

A belt of straw and ivy buds,
With coral clasps and amber studs.
And if these pleasures may thee move,
Come live with me and be my love.

The shepherds' swains shall dance and sing
For thy delight each May morning.
If these delights thy mind may move,
Then live with me and be my love.

CHRISTOPHER MARLOWE

A RED, RED ROSE

O my Luve's like a red, red rose,
That's newly sprung in June:
O my Luve's like the melodie
That's sweetly played in tune!

As fair art thou, my bonnie lass,
So deep in luve am I;
And I will luve thee still, my dear,
Till a' the seas gang dry.

Till a' the seas gang dry, my dear,
And the rocks melt wi' the sun;
I will luve thee still, my dear,
While the sands o' life shall run.

And fare thee weel, my only Luve,
And fare thee weel a while!
And I will come again, my Luve,
Though it were ten thousand mile.

ROBERT BURNS

MY TRUE LOVE HATH MY HEART

My true love hath my heart, and I have his,
By just exchange, one for the other given.
I hold his dear, and mine he cannot miss,
There never was a better bargain driven.
His heart in me keeps me and him in one,
My heart in him his thoughts and senses guides;
He loves my heart, for once it was his own,
I cherish his, because in me it bides.
His heart his wound received from my sight,
My heart was wounded with his wounded heart;
For as from me on him his hurt did light,
So still methought in me his hurt did smart.
Both equal hurt, in this change sought our bliss:
My true love hath my heart and I have his.

SIR PHILIP SIDNEY

A WOMAN'S QUESTION

Before I trust my fate to thee,
Or place my hand in thine,
Before I let thy future give
Color and form to mine,
Before I peril all for thee,
Question thy soul to-night for me.

I break all slighter bonds, nor feel
A shadow of regret:
Is there one link within the past
That holds thy spirit yet?
Or is thy faith as clear and free
As that which I can pledge to thee?

Does there within thy dimmest dreams
A possible future shine,
Wherein thy life could henceforth breathe,
Untouched, unshared by mine?
If so, at any pain or cost,
O, tell me before all is lost!

*   *   *

24

Is there within thy heart a need
That mine cannot fulfil?
One chord that any other hand
Could better wake or still?
Speak now, lest at some future day
My whole life wither and decay.

*   *   *

Couldst thou withdraw thy hand one day
And answer to my claim,
That fate, and that to-day's mistake,–
Not thou,–had been to blame?
Some soothe their conscience thus; but thou
Wilt surely warn and save me now.

Nay, answer *not*,–I dare not hear,
The words would come too late;
Yet I would spare thee all remorse,
So comfort thee, my fate:
Whatever on my heart may fall,
Remember, I *would* risk it all!

ADELAIDE ANNE PROCTER

FAIRER THAN THEE

Fairer than thee, beloved,
Fairer than thee!–
There is one thing, beloved,
Fairer than thee.

Not the glad sun, beloved,
Bright though it beams;
Not the green earth, beloved
Silver with streams;

Not the gay birds, beloved,
Happy and free:
Yet there's one thing, beloved,
Fairer than thee.

Not the clear day, beloved,
Glowing with light;
Not (fairer still, beloved)
Star-crowned night.

Truth in her might, beloved,
Grand in her sway;
Truth with her eyes, beloved,
Clearer than day.

Holy and pure, beloved,
Spotless and free,
Is the one thing, beloved,
Fairer than thee.

Guard well thy soul, beloved;
Truth, dwelling there,
Shall shadow forth, beloved,
Her image rare.

Then shall I deem, beloved,
That thou art she;
And there'll be naught, beloved,
Fairer then thee.

AUTHOR UNKNOWN

MY MISTRESS' EYES ARE NOTHING
LIKE THE SUN

My mistress' eyes are nothing like the sun;
Coral is far more red than her lips' red;
If snow be white, why then her breasts are dun;
If hairs be wires, black wires grow on her head.
I have seen roses damasked, red and white,
But no such roses see I in her cheeks,
And in some perfumes there is more delight
Than in the breath that from my mistress reeks.
I love to hear her speak, yet well I know
That music hath a far more pleasing sound;
I grant I never saw a goddess go:
My mistress when she walks treads on the ground.
And yet by heaven I think my love as rare
As any she belied with false compare.

WILLIAM SHAKESPEARE

NO TIME TO HATE

I had no time to hate, because
The grave would hinder me,
And life was not so ample I
Could finish enmity.

Nor had I time to love, but since
Some industry must be,
The little toil of love, I thought,
Was large enough for me.

EMILY DICKINSON

EARTH TREMBLES WAITING

I wait for his foot fall,
Eager, afraid,
Each evening hour
When the lights fade...

I wait for his voice
To speak low to me—
As a mariner lost
Dreams of harbor, at sea...

I wait for his lips
When the dusk falls.
Life holds my longing
Behind dark walls.

I wait for his face—
As after rain
Earth trembles waiting
For the sun again...

BLANCHE SHOEMAKER WAGSTAFF

LOVE IS NOT ALL: IT IS NOT MEAT
NOR DRINK

Love is not all: it is not meat nor drink
Nor slumber nor a roof against the rain;
Nor yet a floating spar to men that sink
And rise and sink and rise and sink again;
Love cannot fill the thickened lung with breath,
Nor clean the blood, nor set the fractured bone;
Yet many a man is making friends with death
Even as I speak, for lack of love alone.
It well may be that in a difficult hour,
Pinned down by pain and moaning for release,
Or nagged by want past resolution's power,
I might be driven to sell your love for peace,
Or trade the memory of this night for food.
It well may be. I do not think I would.

EDNA ST. VINCENT MILLAY

THE NIGHT-PIECE TO JULIA

Her eyes the glow-worm lend thee,
The shooting stars attend thee;
And the elves also,
Whose little eyes glow
Like the sparks of fire, befriend thee.

No will-o'-th'-wisp mislight thee,
Nor snake or slow-worm bite thee;
But on, on thy way,
Not making a stay,
Since ghost there's none to affright thee.

Let not the dark thee cumber;
What though the moon does slumber?
The stars of the night
Will lend thee their light
Like tapers clear without number.

Then, Julia, let me woo thee,
Thus, thus to come unto me;
And when I shall meet
Thy silv'ry feet
My soul I'll pour into thee.

ROBERT HERRICK

JENNY KISSED ME

Jenny kissed me when we met,
Jumping from the chair she sat in.
Time, you thief, who love to get
Sweets into your list, put that in.
Say I'm weary, say I'm sad;
Say that health and wealth have missed me;
Say I'm growing old, but add–
Jenny kissed me!

LEIGH HUNT

SLY THOUGHTS

"I saw him kiss your cheek!"–
" 'T is true."
"O Modesty!"–" 'T was strictly kept:
He thought me asleep; at least, I knew
He thought I thought he thought I slept."

COVENTRY PATMORE

III.

Love
the
ages
through

SONG

Shall I love you like the wind, love,
That is so fierce and strong,
That sweeps all barriers from its path
And recks not right or wrong?
The passion of the wind, love,
Can never last for long.

Shall I love you like the fire, love,
With furious heat and noise,
To waken in you all love's fears
And little of love's joys?
The passion of the fire, love,
Whate'er it finds; destroys.

I will love you like the stars, love,
Set in the heavenly blue,
That only shine the brighter
After weeping tears of dew;
Above the wind and fire, love,
They love the ages through!

And when this life is o'er, love,
With all its joys and jars,
We'll leave behind the wind and fire
To wage their boisterous wars,—
Then we shall only be, love,
The nearer to the stars!

R. W. RAYMOND

SHE WAS A PHANTOM
OF DELIGHT

She was a phantom of delight
When first she gleamed upon my sight;
A lovely apparition, sent
To be a moment's ornament;
Her eyes as stars of twilight fair;
Like Twilight's, too, her dusky hair;
But all things else about her drawn
From May-time and the cheerful dawn;
A dancing shape, an image gay,
To haunt, to startle, and waylay.

I saw her upon nearer view,
A spirit, yet a woman too!
Her household motions light and free,
And steps of virgin-liberty;
A countenance in which did meet
Sweet records, promises as sweet;
A creature not too bright or good
For human nature's daily food,
For transient sorrows, simple wiles,
Praise, blame, love, kisses, tears, and smiles.

And now I see with eye serene
The very pulse of the machine;
A being breathing thoughtful breath,
A traveller between life and death:
The reason firm, the temperate will,
Endurance, foresight, strength, and skill;
A perfect woman, nobly planned
To warn, to comfort, and command;
And yet a spirit still, and bright
With something of an angel-light.

WILLIAM WORDSWORTH

THE WHITE FLAG

I sent my love two roses,—one
As white as driven snow,
And one a blushing royal red,
A flaming Jacqueminot.

I meant to touch and test my fate;
That night I should divine,
The moment I should see my love,
If her true heart were mine.

For if she holds me dear, I said,
She'll wear my blushing rose;
If not, she'll wear my cold Lamarque,
As white as winter's snows.

My heart sank when I met her: sure
I had been overbold,
For on her breast my pale rose lay
In virgin whiteness cold.

Yet with low words she greeted me,
With smiles divinely tender;
Upon her cheek the red rose dawned,–
The white rose meant surrender.

JOHN HAY

A GIFT

See! I give myself to you, Beloved!
My words are little jars
For you to take and put upon a shelf.
Their shapes are quaint and beautiful,
And they have many pleasant colors and lustres
To recommend them.
Also the scent from them fills the room
With sweetness of flowers and crushed grasses.

When I shall have given you the last one
You will have the whole of me,
But I shall be dead.

AMY LOWELL

LOVE

There are who say the lover's heart
Is in the loved one's merged;
O, never by love's own warm art
So cold a plea was urged!
No!—hearts that love hath crowned or crossed,
Love fondly knits together;
But not a thought or hue is lost
That made a part of either.

*   *   *

It is an ill-told tale that tells
Of "hearts by love made one";
He grows who near another's dwells
More conscious of his own;
In each spring up new thoughts and powers
That, mid love's warm, clear weather,
Together tend like climbing flowers,
And, turning, grow together.

Such fictions blink love's better part,
Yield up its half of bliss;
The wells are in the neighbor heart
When there is thirst in this:
There findeth love the passion-flowers
On which it learns to thrive,
Makes honey in another's bowers,
But brings it home to hive.

Love's life is in its own replies,—
To each low beat it beats,
Smiles back the smiles, sighs back the sighs,
And every throb repeats.
Then, since one loving heart still throws
Two shadows in love's sun,
How should two loving hearts compose
And mingle into one?

THOMAS KIBBLE HERVEY

THE FIRST TIME

The first time that the sun rose on thine oath
To love me, I looked forward to the moon
To slacken all those bonds which seemed too soon
And quickly tied to make a lasting troth.
Quick-loving hearts, I thought, may quickly loathe;
And, looking on myself, I seemed not one
For such man's love!—more like an out of tune
Worn viol, a good singer would be wroth
To spoil his song with, and which, snatched in haste
Is laid down at the first ill-sounding note.
I did not wrong myself so, but I placed
A wrong on *thee*. For perfect strains may float
Neath master-hands, from instruments defaced,—
And great souls, at one stroke, may do and doat.

ELIZABETH BARRETT BROWNING

MARRIAGE
FROM "HUMAN LIFE"

Then before All they stand,—the holy vow
And ring of gold, no fond illusions now,
Bind her as his. Across the threshold led,
And every tear kissed off as soon as shed,
His house she enters,—there to be a light,
Shining within, when all without is night;
A guardian angel o'er his life presiding,
Doubling his pleasures and his cares dividing,
Winning him back when mingling in the throng,
Back from a world we love, alas! too long,
To fireside happiness, to hours of ease,
Blest with that charm, the certainty to please.
How oft her eyes read his; her gentle mind
To all his wishes, all his thoughts inclined;
Still subject,—ever on the watch to borrow
Mirth of his mirth and sorrow of his sorrow!
The soul of music slumbers in the shell,
Till waked and kindled by the master's spell,
And feeling hearts—touch them but rightly—pour
A thousand melodies unheard before!

SAMUEL ROGERS

THE NEWLYWEDS

"What is the thing your eyes hold loveliest
In these, our fields and shores? I'll bring it home."
With tenderness, awaiting her request,
He stood. The dooryard dogwood was a foam
Of wind-tipped flowers, catching at her breath,
But these she did not mention, trying hard
To meet his eagerness. "Come flood, or death
By thunderbolt," he laughed, "I'll heap the yard
With everything you ask for. Name it now."
She made no answer, yet a little smile
Marked for him her compliance. Then, the bough
Tilted its stiffened beauty like a pile
Of snowy cloud above them. "Ah, I know,"
He cried, "Your heart is set on something far
Beyond our present means. Is that not so?"

"I want you and the dogwood as you are,
April forever. Can you heap that here?"
And while she watched, the boy went out of him.
"I think I understand your wifely fear,"
And, reaching up, he shook a weighted limb.
So, like the blossoms, quiet settled there.
"I will not run away to bring you gifts."
He spoke less lightly. "Boys can never bear
The undramatic thing. Their rich blood lifts
Their spirits higher than their hands, but men
May learn where such as you will teach,
How life is spent at try and try again
To keep white-blowing loveliness in reach."

CLOYD MANN CRISWELL

THE POET'S SONG TO HIS WIFE

How many summers, love,
Have I been thine?
How many days, thou dove,
Hast thou been mine?
Time, like the winged wind
When 't bends the flowers,
Hath left no mark behind,
To count the hours!

Some weight of thought, though loath,
On thee he leaves;
Some lines of care round both
Perhaps he weaves;
Some fears,—a soft regret
For joys scarce known;
Sweet looks we half forget;—
All else is flown!

Ah!–With what thankless heart
I mourn and sing!
Look, where our children start,
Like sudden spring!
With tongues all sweet and low
Like a pleasant rhyme,
They tell how much I owe
To thee and time!

BARRY CORNWALL

COME, REST IN THIS BOSOM
FROM "IRISH MELODIES"

Come, rest in this bosom, my own stricken deer,
Though the herd have fled from thee, thy home is still
    here;
Here still is the smile, that no cloud can o'ercast,
And a heart and a hand all thy own to the last.

Oh! what was love made for, if 't is not the same
Through joy and through torment, through glory and
    shame?
I know not, I ask not, if guilt's in that heart,
I but know that I love thee, whatever thou art.

Thou hast called me thy Angel in moments of bliss,
And thy Angel I'll be, mid the horrors of this,
Through the furnace, unshrinking, thy steps to pursue,
And shield thee, and save thee,—or perish there too!

THOMAS MOORE

A WISH

Mine be a cot beside the hill;
A bee-hive's hum shall soothe my ear;
A willowy brook that turns a mill,
With many a fall shall linger near.

The swallow, oft, beneath my thatch
Shall twitter from her clay-built nest;
Oft shall the pilgrim lift the latch,
And share my meal, a welcome guest.

Around my ivied porch shall spring
Each fragrant flower that drinks the dew;
And Lucy, at her wheel, shall sing
In russet gown and apron blue.

The village-church among the trees,
Where first our marriage-vows were given,
With merry peals shall swell the breeze
And point with taper spire to heaven.

SAMUEL ROGERS

HOW DO I LOVE THEE?
LET ME COUNT THE WAYS

How do I love thee? Let me count the ways.
I love thee to the depth and breadth and height
My soul can reach, when feeling out of sight
For the ends of Being and ideal Grace.
I love thee to the level of every day's
Most quiet need; by sun and candle-light.
I love thee freely, as men strive for Right;
I love thee purely, as they turn from Praise.
I love thee with the passion put to use
In my old griefs, and with my childhood's faith.
I love thee with a love I seemed to lose
With my lost saints,—I love thee with the breath,
Smiles, tears, of all my life!—and, if God choose,
I shall but love thee better after death.

ELIZABETH BARRETT BROWNING

UPON THE SAND

All love that has not friendship for its base,
Is like a mansion built upon the sand.
Though brave its walls as any in the land,
And its tall turrets lift their heads in grace;
Though skillful and accomplished artists trace
Most beautiful designs on every hand,
And gleaming statues in dim niches stand,
And fountains play in some flow'r-hidden place:

Yet, when from the frowning east a sudden gust
Of adverse fate is blown, or sad rains fall
Day in, day out, against its yielding wall,
Lo! the fair structure crumbles to the dust.
Love, to endure life's sorrow and earth's woe,
Needs friendship's solid masonwork below.

ELLA WHEELER WILCOX

THE FIRESIDE

Dear Chloe, while the busy crowd,
The vain, the wealthy, and the proud,
In folly's maze advance;
Though singularity and pride
Be called our choice, we'll step aside,
Nor join the giddy dance.

From the gay world we'll oft retire
To our own family and fire,
Where love our hours employs;
No noisy neighbor enters here,
No intermeddling stranger near,
To spoil our heartfelt joys.

If solid happiness we prize,
Within our breast this jewel lies,
And they are fools who roam;
The world hath nothing to bestow,–
From our own selves our bliss must flow,
And that dear hut, our home.

Our portion is not large, indeed;
But then how little do we need,
For nature's calls are few;
In this the art of living lies,
To want no more than may suffice,
And make that little do.

We'll therefore relish with content
Whate'er kind Providence has sent,
Nor aim beyond our power;
For, if our stock be very small,
'T is prudence to enjoy it all,
Nor lose the present hour.

To be resigned when ills betide,
Patient when favors are denied,
And pleased with favors given,—
Dear Chloe, this is wisdom's part,
This is that incense of the heart,
Whose fragrance smells to heaven.

NATHANIEL COTTON

O, LAY THY HAND IN MINE, DEAR!

O, lay thy hand in mine, dear!
We're growing old;
But Time hath brought no sign, dear,
That hearts grow cold.
'T is long, long since our new love
Made life divine;
But age enricheth true love,
Like noble wine.

*   *   *

O, lean thy life on mine, dear!
'T will shelter thee.
Thou wert a winsome vine, dear,
On my young tree:
And so, till boughs are leafless,
And songbirds flown,
We'll twine, then lay us, griefless,
Together down.

GERALD MASSEY

THE FIRE OF DRIFT-WOOD
DEVEREAUX FARM, NEAR MARBLEHEAD

We sat within the farm-house old,
Whose windows, looking o'er the bay,
Gave to the sea-breeze damp and cold
An easy entrance, night and day.

Not far away we saw the port,
The strange, old-fashioned, silent town,
The lighthouse, the dismantled fort,
The wooden houses, quaint and brown.

We sat and talked until the night,
Descending, filled the little room;
Our faces faded from the sight,
Our voices only broke the gloom.

We spake of many a vanished scene,
Of what we once had thought and said,
Of what had been, and might have been,
And who was changed, and who was dead;

And all that fills the hearts of friends,
When first they feel, with secret pain,
Their lives thenceforth have separate ends,
And never can be one again;

The first slight swerving of the heart,
That words are powerless to express,
And leave it still unsaid in part,
Or say it in too great excess.

The very tones in which we spake
Had something strange, I could but mark;
The leaves of memory seemed to make
A mournful rustling in the dark.

Oft died the words upon our lips,
As suddenly, from out the fire
Built of the wreck of stranded ships,
The flames would leap and then expire.

And, as their splendor flashed and failed,
We thought of wrecks upon the main,
Of ships dismasted, that were hailed
And sent no answer back again.

The windows, rattling in their frames,
The ocean, roaring up the beach,
The gusty blast, the bickering flames,
All mingled vaguely in our speech;

Until they made themselves a part
Of fancies floating through the brain,
The long-lost ventures of the heart,
That send no answers back again.

O flames that glowed! O hearts that yearned!
They were indeed too much akin,
The drift-wood fire without that burned,
The thoughts that burned and glowed within.

HENRY WADSWORTH LONGFELLOW

CONNUBIAL LIFE
FROM "THE SEASONS"

But happy they! the happiest of their kind!
Whom gentler stars unite, and in one fate
Their hearts, their fortunes, and their beings blend,
'T is not the coarser tie of human laws,
Unnatural oft, and foreign to the mind,
That binds their peace, but harmony itself,
Attuning all their passions into love;
Where friendship full-exerts her softest power,
Perfect esteem enlivened by desire
Ineffable, and sympathy of soul;
Thought meeting thought, and will preventing will,
With boundless confidence: for naught but love
Can answer love, and render bliss secure.
Meantime a smiling offspring rises round,
And mingles both their graces. By degrees,
The human blossom blows; and ever day,
Soft as it rolls along, shows some new charm,
The father's lustre and the mother's bloom.
Then infant reason grows apace, and calls
For the kind hand of an assiduous care.
Delightful task! to rear the tender thought,
To teach the young idea how to shoot,

To pour the fresh instruction o'er the mind,
To breathe the enlivening spirit, and to fix
The generous purpose in the glowing breast.
O, speak the joy! ye whom the sudden tear
Surprises often, while you look around,
And nothing strikes your eye but sights of bliss,
All various Nature pressing on the heart;
An elegant sufficiency, content,
Retirement, rural quiet, friendship, books,
Ease and alternate labor, useful life,
Progressive virtue, and approving Heaven.
These are the matchless joys of virtuous love;
And thus their moments fly. The Seasons thus,
As ceaseless round a jarring world they roll,
Still find them happy; and consenting Spring
Sheds her rosy garland on their heads:
Till evening comes at last, serene and mild;
When after the long vernal day of life,
Enamored more, as more remembrance swells
With many a proof of recollected love,
Together down they sink in social sleep;
Together freed, their gentle spirits fly
To scenes where love and bliss immortal reign.

JAMES THOMSON

THE WORN WEDDING-RING

Your wedding-ring wears thin, dear wife; ah, summers not a
   few,
Since I put it on your finger first, have passed o'er me and
   you;
And, love, what changes we have seen,—what cares and
   pleasures, too,—
Since you became my own dear wife, when this old ring was
   new!

O, blessings on that happy day, the happiest of my life,
When, thanks to God, your low, sweet "Yes" made you my
   loving wife!
Your heart will say the same, I know; that day's as dear to
   you,—
That day that made me yours, dear wife, when this old ring
   was new.

How well do I remember now your young sweet face that
   day!
How fair you were, how dear you were, my tongue could
   hardly say;
Nor how I doated on you; O, how proud I was of you!
But did I love you more than now, when this old ring was
   new?

No—no! no fairer were you then than at this hour to me;
And, dear as life to me this day, how could you dearer be?
As sweet your face might be that day as now it is, 't is true;
But did I know your heart as well when this old ring was
    new?

O partner of my gladness, wife, what care, what grief is
    there
For me you would not bravely face, with me you would not
    share?
O, what a weary want had every day, if wanting you,
Wanting the love that God made mine when this old ring
    was new!

Years bring fresh links to bind us, wife,—young voices that
    are here;
Young faces round our fire that make their mother's yet
    more dear;
Young loving hearts your care each day makes yet more like
    to you,
More like the loving heart made mine when this old ring
    was new.

And blessed be God! all he has given are with us yet;
  around
Our table every precious life lent to us still is found.
Though cares we've known, with hopeful hearts
  the worst we've struggled through;
Blessed be his name for all his love since this old ring was
  new!

The past is dear, its sweetness still our memories treasure
  yet;
The griefs we've borne, together borne, we would not now
  forget.
Whatever, wife, the future brings, heart unto heart still true,
We'll share as we have shared all else since this old ring was
  new.

And if God spare us 'mongst our sons and daughters to
  grow old,
We know his goodness will not let your heart or mine grow
  cold.
Your aged eyes will see in mine all they've still shown to
  you,
And mine in yours all they have seen since this old ring
  was new.

And O, when death shall come at last to bid me to
    my rest,
May I die looking in those eyes, and resting on that
    breast;
O, may my parting gaze be blessed with the dear sight of
    you,
Of those fond eyes,–fond as they were when this
    old ring was new!

WILLIAM COX BENNETT

IV.

Love is to the farthest place

❧

ONE DAY I WROTE HER NAME
UPON THE STRAND

One day I wrote her name upon the strand;
But came the waves, and washed it away:
Again, I wrote it with a second hand;
But came the tide, and made my pains his prey.
Vain man, said she, that dost in vain assay
A mortal thing so to immortalize;
For I myself shall like to this decay,
And eke my name be wiped out likewise.
Not so, quoth I; let baser things devise
To die in dust, but you shall live by fame:
My verse your virtues rare shall eternize,
And in the heavens write your glorious name.
Where, whenas death shall all the world subdue,
Our love shall live, and later life renew.

EDMUND SPENSER

WE PARTED IN SILENCE

We parted in silence, we parted by night,
On the banks of that lonely river;
Where the fragrant limes their boughs unite,
We met—and we parted forever!
The night-bird sung, and the stars above
Told many a touching story,
Of friends long passed to the kingdom of love,
Where the soul wears its mantle of glory.

*　　*　　*

And now on the midnight sky I look,
And my heart grows full of weeping;
Each star is to me a sealed book,
Some tale of that loved one keeping.
We parted in silence,—we parted in tears,
On the banks of that lovely river:
But the odor and bloom of those bygone years
Shall hang o'er its waters forever.

MRS. CRAWFORD

SWEETEST LOVE, I DO NOT GO

Sweetest love, I do not go
For weariness of thee,
Nor in hope the world can show
A fitter love for me;
But since that I
Must die at last, 'tis best
To use myself in jest
Thus by feigned deaths to die.

Yesternight the sun went hence,
And yet is here today;
He hath no desire nor sense,
Nor half so short a way.
Then fear not me,
But believe that I shall make
Speedier journeys, since I take
More wings and spurs than he.

O how feeble is man's power,
That, if good fortune fall,
Cannot add another hour
Nor a lost hour recall!

But come bad chance,
And we join to it our strength,
And we teach it art and length,
Itself o'er us to advance.

When thou sigh'st thou sigh'st not wind,
But sigh'st my soul away;
When thou weep'st, unkindly kind,
My life's blood doth decay.
It cannot be
That thou lov'st me as thou say'st,
If in thine my life thou waste:
That art the best of me.

Let not thy divining heart
Forethink me any ill;
Destiny may take thy part,
And may thy fears fulfil.
But think that we
Are but turned aside to sleep:
They who one another keep
Alive, ne'er parted be.

JOHN DONNE

THE WIFE TO HER HUSBAND

Linger not long. Home is not home without thee:
Its dearest tokens do but make me mourn.
O, let its memory, like a chain about thee,
Gently compel and hasten thy return!

Linger not long. Though crowds should woo thy staying,
Bethink thee, can the mirth of thy friends, though dear,
Compensate for the grief thy long delaying
Costs the fond heart that sighs to have thee here?

Linger not long. How shall I watch thy coming,
As evening shadows stretch o'er moor and dell;
When the wild bee hath ceased her busy humming,
And silence hangs on all things like a spell!

How shall I watch for thee, when fears grow stronger,
As night grows dark and darker on the hill!
How shall I weep, when I can watch no longer!
Ah! art thou absent, art thou absent still?

Yet I should grieve not, though the eye that seeth me
Gazeth through tears that make its splendor dull;
For oh! I sometimes fear when thou art with me,
My cup of happiness is all too full.

Haste, haste thee home to thy mountain dwelling,
Haste, as a bird unto its peaceful nest!
Haste, as a skiff, through tempests wide and swelling,
Flies to its haven of securest rest!

AUTHOR UNKNOWN

ABSENCE

What shall I do with all the days and hours
That must be counted ere I see thy face?
How shall I charm the interval that lowers
Between this time and that sweet time of grace?

Shall I in slumber steep each weary sense,—
Weary with longing? Shall I flee away
Into past days, and with some fond pretence
Cheat myself to forget the present day?

Shall love for thee lay on my soul the sin
Of casting from me God's great gift of time?
Shall I, these mists of memory locked within,
Leave and forget life's purposes sublime?

O, how or by what means may I contrive
To bring the hour that brings thee back more near?
How may I teach my drooping hope to live
Until that blessed time, and thou art here?

I'll tell thee; for thy sake I will lay hold
Of all good aims, and consecrate to thee,
In worthy deeds, each moment that is told
While thou, beloved one! art far from me.

For thee I will arouse my thoughts to try
All heavenward flights, all high and holy strains;
For thy dear sake I will walk patiently
Through these long hours, nor call their minutes pains.

I will this dreary blank of absence make
A noble task-time; and will therein strive
To follow excellence, and to o'ertake
More good than I have won since yet I live.

So may this doomed time build up in me
A thousand graces, which shall thus be thine;
So may my love and longing hallowed be,
And thy dear thought an influence divine.

FRANCES ANNE KEMBLE

TO HER ABSENT SAILOR
FROM "THE TENT ON THE BEACH"

Her window opens to the bay,
On glistening light or misty gray,
And there at dawn and set of day
In prayer she kneels:
"Dear Lord!" she saith, "to many a home
From wind and wave the wanderers come;
I only see the tossing foam
Of stranger keels.

"Blown out and in by summer gales,
The stately ships, with crowded sails,
And sailors leaning o'er their rails,
Before me glide;
They come, they go, but nevermore,
Spice-laden from the Indian shore,
I see his swift-winged Isidore
The waves divide.

*   *   *

"O dread and cruel deep, reveal
The secret which thy waves conceal,
And, ye wild sea-birds, hither wheel
And tell your tale.

Let winds that tossed his raven hair
A message from my lost one bear,–
Some thought of me, a last fond prayer
Or dying wail!

"Come, with your dreariest truth shut out
The fears that haunt me round about;
O God! I cannot bear this doubt
That stifles breath.
The worst is better than the dread;
Give me but leave to mourn my dead
Asleep in trust and hope, instead
Of life in death!"

It might have been the evening breeze
That whispered in the garden trees,
It might have been the sound of seas
That rose and fell;
But, with her heart, if not her ear,
The old loved voice she seemed to hear:
"I wait to meet thee: be of cheer
For all is well!"

JOHN GREENLEAF WHITTIER

SUMMER DAYS

In summer, when the days were long,
We walked together in the wood:
Our heart was light, our step was strong;
Sweet flutterings were there in our blood,
In summer, when the days were long.

We strayed from morn till evening came;
We gathered flowers, and wove us crowns;
We walked mid poppies red as flame,
Or sat upon the yellow downs;
And always wished our life the same.

In summer, when the days were long,
We leaped the hedgerow, crossed the brook;
And still her voice flowed forth in song,
Or else she read some graceful book,
In summer, when the days were long.

And then we sat beneath the trees,
With shadows lessening in the noon;
And in the sunlight and the breeze,
We feasted, many a gorgeous June,
While larks were singing o'er the leas.

*   *   *

We loved, and yet we knew it not,—
For loving seemed like breathing then;
We found a heaven in every spot;
Saw angels, too, in all good men;
And dreamed of God in grove and grot.

In summer, when the days were long,
Alone I wander, muse alone.
I see her not; but that old song
Under the fragrant wind is blown,
In summer, when the days are long.

Alone I wander in the wood:
But one fair spirit hears my sighs;
And half I see, so glad and good,
The honest daylight of her eyes,
That charmed me under earlier skies.

In summer, when the days are long,
I love her as we loved of old.
My heart is light, my step is strong;
For love brings back those hours of gold,
In summer, when the days are long.

AUTHOR UNKNOWN

A LITTLE WHILE I FAIN
WOULD LINGER YET

A little while (my life is almost set!)
I fain would pause along the downward way,
Musing an hour in this sad sunset ray,
While, Sweet! our eyes with tender tears are wet:
A little hour I fain would linger yet.

A little while I fain would linger yet,
All for love's sake, for love that cannot tire;
Though fervid youth be dead, with youth's desire,
And hope had faded to a vague regret,
A little while I fain would linger yet.

A little while I fain would linger here:
Behold! who knows what strange, mysterious bars
'Twixt souls that love may rise in other stars?
Nor can love deem the face of death is fair:
A little while I still would linger here.

*   *   *

A little while, when light and twilight meet,–
Behind, our broken years; before, the deep
Weird wonder of the last unfathomed sleep,–
A little while I still would clasp thee, Sweet,
A little while, when night and twilight meet.

A little while I fain would linger here;
Behold! who knows what soul-dividing bars
Earth's faithful loves may part in other stars?
Nor can love deem the face of death is fair:
A little while I still would linger here.

PAUL HAMILTON HAYNE

THE UNQUIET GRAVE

"The wind doth blow today, my love,
And a few small drops of rain;
I never had but one true love,
In cold grave she was lain.

"I'll do as much for my true love
As any young man may;
I'll sit and mourn all at her grave
For a twelvemonth, and a day."

"The twelvemonth and a day being up,
The dead began to speak,
"Oh who sits weeping on my grave,
And will not let me sleep?"

"'Tis I, my love, sits on your grave
And will not let you sleep,
For I crave one kiss of your clay-cold lips
And that is all I seek."

"You crave one kiss of clay-cold lips,
But my breath smells earthy strong;
If you have one kiss of my clay-cold lips
Your time will not be long:

"'Tis down in yonder garden green,
Love, where we used to walk,
The finest flower that ere was seen
Is withered to a stalk.

"The stalk is withered dry, my love,
So will our hearts decay;
So make yourself content, my love,
Till God calls you away."

AUTHOR UNKNOWN

A FAREWELL

With all my will, but much against my heart,
We two now part.
My Very Dear,
Our solace is, the sad road lies so clear.
It needs no art,
With faint, averted feet
And many a tear,
In our opposed paths to persevere.
Go thou to East, I West.
We will not say
There's any hope, it is so far away.
But, O my Best,
When the one darling of our widowhead,
The nursing Grief,
Is dead,

And no dews blur our eyes
To see the peach-bloom come in evening skies,
Perchance we may,
Where now this night is day,
And even through faith of still averted feet,
Making full circle of our banishment,
Amazed meet;
The bitter journey to the bourne so sweet
Seasoning the termless feast of our content
With tears of recognition never dry.

COVENTRY PATMORE

AND I AM OLD TO KNOW

No place seemed farther than your death
but when I went there—gone from there,
it was from your love you spoke
and it was to your love I moved.

And as you speak it—you, my own:
in the days, in the nights of your voice,
always the word of love opens,
opens into all its meaning.

And as I longer move to you,
as you wait and as you take me,
not like a lover but like love
you tell me and I am old to know:

love is to the farthest place—
love is to so far a place
from always its greatest distances,
to see where death was, I look back.

PAULINE HANSON

SWEET LOVE, RENEW THY FORCE

Sweet love, renew thy force; be it not said
Thy edge should blunter be than appetite,
Which but today by feeding is allay'd,
Tomorrow sharpen'd in his former might.
So, love, be thou; although today thou fill
Thy hungry eyes even till they wink with fullness,
Tomorrow see again, and do not kill
The spirit of love with a perpetual dullness.
Let this sad int'rim like the ocean be
Which parts the shore where two contracted new
Come daily to the banks, that, when they see
Return of love, more blest may be the view;
Or call it winter, which, being full of care,
Makes summer's welcome thrice more wish'd, more rare.

WILLIAM SHAKESPEARE

SONG
FROM "TORRISMOND"

How many times do I love thee, dear?
Tell me how many thoughts there be
In the atmosphere
Of a new-fall'n year,
Whose white and sable hours appear
The latest flake of Eternity:
So many times do I love thee, dear.

How many times do I love again?
Tell me how many beads there are
In a silver chain
Of evening rain,
Unravelled from the tumbling main,
And threading the eye of a yellow star:
So many times do I love thee again.

THOMAS LOVELL BEDDOES